La Cascada

William D. Van Atta Jr.

Dedication

To my mom, dad, three brothers, and three sisters, for all their loving support over the years. To the many precious furry and winged companions I have had the honor of experiencing life with.

Acknowledgment

I would like to give special thanks to my mom, who introduced me to the poems of her grandfather, Joseph Russell Taylor, and his acquaintance, Robert W. Service. Thank you to the many teachers who patiently helped me with my deficient reading and writing skills.

For introducing me to the North Woods, I would like to thank the Whiteways—Dr. Robert (Red) and his wife, Marion. I worked my way through college as the Whiteways' handyman.

About the Author

William (Bill) D. Van Atta Jr. is a veteran Army aviator and retired registered nurse who is a native of the Midwest, now living in La Crescent, Minnesota. Bill holds a Bachelor of Science degree in geography from the University of Wisconsin–La Crosse.

After 12 years of service in the U.S. Army as both a rotary-wing and fixed-wing aviator, Bill went back to school. He graduated from The Norfolk General Hospital School of Nursing and then completed his Bachelor of Science in Nursing degree at Excelsior University and was licensed as an RN.

Bill practiced in several hospitals, including Level 1 and Level 2 trauma centers, where he specialized in the care of surgical, trauma, and burn patients.

When not writing, Bill enjoys spending time with his dogs. He especially likes being outdoors—camping, hiking, and photographing nature. Over the past couple of years, Bill has been putting his woodworking skills to the test building a small sailboat. He is an avid swimmer and has competed in several open water swimming competitions.

You can connect with Bill at: running_wolf57@yahoo.com

Within a matter of hours, we had leapfrogged south, leaving the sub-zero February cold of La Crosse, Wisconsin, for the warm tropics of the Dominican Republic. We spent the night at El Embajador Hotel in Santo Domingo, and now Dick Keller's King Air, loaded with scuba gear and anxious adventurers, left the ground and headed north for the town of Mao.

Flying the plane was Dick, owner of Keller Rock and Lime. I believe he said he was a crew member on a B-17 bomber in World War II. In the seat to the right of Dick sat an old Black man, Bill Richards. Bill, a native of the Dominican Republic, had recently returned to the country. He was a mining superintendent before he left years ago during the revolution, fearing for his life.

In the seat behind Dick was Dean Phillips, owner of a gas company in Iowa. From what we were told, his business took him from rags to riches. Dean picked us up in his Cessna twin-engine airplane two days ago in La Crosse and flew us to his home in Iowa, which had a private airstrip. After landing and sliding down the snow-covered runway, he taxied the plane to the hangar next to his home, where we spent the first night.

In the back of the plane, among the scuba tanks, picks, shovels, and black plastic sampling bags, sat my dad, Dr. William Van Atta

Sr., a college professor, and myself, William Jr., a college student and amateur photographer. My dad, a master dive instructor, and I were asked by Jim Silvy, owner of another gas company, to take bottom samples from a small pool in the Cordillera Central Mountains. The pool was fed by a 300-foot vertical falls known as Salto de Jicomé. This waterfall is one of the highest in the country.

There was gold in the pool and along the river, but Silvy and his friends wanted to know if there was enough to make mining profitable. We were told that the river and pool were panned and worked previously with some success. It is believed that the ancient native people took gold from the river before the invasion of the Spaniards. It was rumored that the spirit of a chief haunted the falls.

During the early 1950s, an American had taken gold from the pool, but his equipment was destroyed by floods, and he left the country.

Jim was in a second plane, along with Mort Walker, a wheat farmer with 10,000 acres in Australia. Also onboard was Merlin Savage, who told us he was a bodyguard to General Douglas MacArthur in WWII. Merlin had recently arranged a large oil deal between Kuwait and the Dominican Republic. The remaining passengers were a mechanical engineer, a doctor, and our host, Ron Ortez, Treasurer of Santo Domingo. Ron met us on arrival to the country and used his connections to whisk us through the airport, bypassing customs.

We were almost there. Dick and Mort were on the lookout for the tiny field on which we were to land. They didn't look long when a crop duster appeared, flew up, and guided us onto the landing strip.

We were soon on the ground, unloading all the equipment needed for our trip to the falls. There were many people watching and helping. A small building stood at the edge of the field. In front of it were two armed soldiers. A gold Ford LTD was parked just inside the building. We soon learned that the car belonged to the provincial general, General Oliverez. The car was a gift from President Balaguer. The general met us at the airfield, and we all shook his hand while his bodyguards watched closely.

After some friendly chatting, we climbed into three cars and sped down the rough gravel road toward town. Along the road were several laborers working in large green fields of rice and tobacco.

We bounced off the gravel onto the blacktop of Mao and pulled up to the Hotel Cahoba. The General's car arrived first. In the entrance of the hotel, I could see his bodyguards dressed in camouflaged jungle fatigues, checking the area. They both had automatic weapons. One had a Thompson submachine gun, and the other had an Israeli-made Uzi machine pistol. They looked at my dad and me with suspicion.

When we were all in the lobby, we checked in, then headed for the dining room and lunch. After eating, we retired to our rooms for showers and a nap.

It was getting dark as Dad and I emerged from our room. We walked out to the patio, where Ron, Bill, and some of the others were enjoying drinks in the tropical air. Adjacent to the patio was the swimming pool, which was half-filled with greenish water. The patio and pool were surrounded by a rock wall with jagged pieces of colored glass embedded in the top, serving as a barrier for trespassers.

The waiter went to get me a Coke and my dad a beer. As he returned, the General's car rolled into the drive. His guards checked the area, and then the General and all the investors entered for a conference in a small room next to the pool.

Within five minutes, they reemerged, then left the hotel with the General in two waiting cars. Bill told us that the General had invited them to his house. They had evidently asked the General to join their group. This was necessary if they wished to be active in his province.

Gold was only a secondary reason for the investors' interest in the Dominican Republic. Their primary interest was in the purchase of an undeveloped oceanside resort in Samina. It was during an earlier trip related to the resort that they learned of the gold and decided to check it out. Because some of the men had not seen the resort yet, they decided to look it over before returning home.

Bill, the engineer, my dad, and I had not been alone long when the gold LTD reappeared in the driveway. The General's two bodyguards emerged and approached us. They talked with Bill, and then he translated for us. He said we were all to go to the General's home.

We all got up and went to the car. As I sat down in the back seat, I saw the machine pistol belonging to a guard lying on the floor between my legs. He retrieved it, then sat down in the front seat next to the driver. The driver slammed his door and accelerated down the driveway onto the dark road. He drove wildly down the narrow streets and stopped in front of a darkened three-story, flat-topped building.

The guard and driver stepped from the car. They told us to wait, then walked across the street into the dark stairwell. After a few moments, one of them returned to lead us up the stairs. The guard walked in front of us with weapon in hand to check the flights of stairs ahead. We had to stop at each floor while he checked ahead. We passed the third floor and stepped onto the roof.

Jim, Dick, and the others were all there, relaxing with drinks in hand. After about an hour of talking, drinking, and planning, it was time to leave. Two of the General's men drove four of us back to the hotel and then later returned with the others. We then walked into town for some dinner.

After dinner, we returned to the hotel for some much-needed sleep. Tomorrow at 5:00 AM, we would leave for the waterfall. We were told it was only a short distance; however, it would take several hours to get there on the mountain roads and paths.

With thoughts of the past day's activity, I drifted off into a deep sleep, not knowing that tomorrow's trip to the waterfall would be one of the most interesting and adventurous days of the trip—and of my life.

At 5:00 AM, the phone rang, ending our rest. My dad and I climbed out of our beds, got dressed, then headed to the dining room for a quick breakfast. It was not long before several four-wheel drive vehicles arrived to transport us to the waterfall.

Dawn was just breaking when we finally got loaded up and started our journey. My dad and I rode in the back of a green Toyota Jeep. The caravan traveled down the paved road, then after a few miles veered right onto a very rough dirt road. We held on and felt every bump shaking our bones.

We had not gone far when we came to a halt. The road ahead was underwater and appeared to be impassable. We exited the Jeep and walked along the dry ground while the drivers, one by one, took a try at driving through the mud. One vehicle got stuck and had to be pulled free.

Now clear of the muddy obstacle, we climbed back into the vehicles and continued down the winding backroads. After what seemed like hours, we arrived at the river, only to find that the bridge crossing had been washed out.

Within a few minutes, we were loading a small ferry that crossed the river adjacent to the bridge. A rope was strung across the water and anchored to trees on either side. The boat was pulled across the river by the boat's operator.

We climbed aboard the ferry, and after several trips, everyone and all the equipment made it to the other side.

The rest of the trek would be on foot. Burros carried all our equipment. Our escorts for this part of the journey were two armed soldiers.

It was now time to start the hike to the waterfall. The trail was close to the river and passed many small farms. There were people of all ages along the trail. They always gave a friendly wave as we walked along.

The trail slowly got steeper and narrower, and some of the out-of-shape businessmen started to struggle. The local guides fashioned some walking sticks for us to help on the uneven terrain. We took several breaks, stopping at a few farms where we would rest.

At one farm, the soldiers picked some wild mangos. They cut them up and shared them with the group. I had never eaten or even known about mangos. I took a bite of the juicy fruit and found it quite refreshing.

Soon the break was over, and we were back on the never-ending trail. We found ourselves crossing the river several times and then followed it the remainder of the way to the falls.

We had been walking for three or four hours now, and everyone was getting tired. We were all ill-prepared for the excursion. Some of the men were dressed in casual business attire and street shoes. One was even wearing a leather jacket and cowboy boots. We carried no water, no food, and only had the clothes on our backs.

Soon, the parade of Americans came to a halt. A soldier came from up ahead and told us we were close. He pointed up the trail, shouting, "La Cascada! La Cascada!"

In the distance, we could hear the low rumble of Salto De Jicome's cascading waters. As we moved forward, we could feel the cool, misty breath of the falls. Occasionally, we could look up and see it through breaks in the forest canopy.

We emerged from the vegetation, and there it was—the magnificent waterfall. You couldn't capture the beauty of the falls in a single glance. You had to scan it, looking up and down. As if alive, the water danced its way down the rock face to the pool below. Wisps of windblown mist were cast through the air, dropping the temperature considerably. We all stood and watched for several minutes, hypnotized by its spirit.

It was now getting late, and we had to get to work sampling the pool. We quickly unpacked the burros and set up our gear on the beach near the pool.

Everyone gathered to brief on the plan for collecting the samples. After the brief, my dad and I suited up and prepared to enter the water.

I stepped into the pool first. I was tethered to a line that my dad tended. We used the line for safety and as a guide to help us decide where to take a sample. We alternated between diving and tending. We worked our way around the circumference of the pool, taking samples every 10 feet. We finished in a couple of hours with about 60 samples. The samples were about one gallon each and placed into black garbage bags.

By the time we left the water and changed out of our gear, it was early evening, and we were falling under the shadow of the mountain. As it started to get dark, it was decided that it was best to remain at the falls until morning instead of risking travel at night.

The mountain air grew cooler, and then one of the guides got a fire going. Word of our presence traveled fast, and soon some of the local people showed up with chicken and rice to share with us. It was a welcoming treat for our hungry bellies.

With our bellies full, we started to think about sleep. We had no sleeping bags and no blankets. Our dilemma was trying to figure out how to sleep and stay warm. After considering our limited options, we decided the only thing to do was to make use of the black garbage bags we had. It was then that we decided to use the bags as sleeping bags. Yes, we ended up sleeping in garbage bags.

It was a long night. Needless to say, the black plastic garbage bags provided no warmth. They did provide some protection from the damp, misty air of the falls. The night passed slowly. At first light, I awoke cold and in the fetal position. One by one, we emerged from the black bags and made our way to the fire. I don't recall if there was anything to eat, but there was coffee that one of the guides made. It was mixed with honey and passed around in an old bottle. I slowly warmed up in the sunshine and prepared for the return trip.

For the trip back, we broke into two groups. One group would go with the burros, all the equipment, and the samples on the trail that brought us in. The second group would go back by way of the upper falls. This route would involve some steep, slippery climbing. My dad and I were in this group along with Jim, Dean, Ron, a soldier, and a guide.

We got underway and started our climb up the muddy hillside to the left of the falls. We watched as the other group started their return down the trail. Grabbing hold of vegetation, we pulled ourselves hand over hand up the side of the waterfall until we reached the top. We rested and took in the view of the valley below.

Up top, we saw evidence of some small concrete dams and shoots aimed at redirecting the water flow. These were probably built by the American who worked the area years ago. Continuing up the river, we walked until joining the trail that would take us to the vehicles and the comfort of the hotel.

This new route took us across the high ground. We continued to come upon many small farms and friendly people.

Occasionally we could see the river and its rapids in the valley below.

After a couple of hours of walking, we made it to the waiting vehicles. Within a few minutes, the other group arrived. They rode the ferry across the river to join us.

All loaded up, we took our seats and drove back to Mao. At the hotel, we got cleaned up, had a quick lunch, checked out, and then headed back to the airfield.

Everything was routine from here. We flew back to Santo Domingo. Then, after a night of rest, we flew back to La Crosse and the cold of winter.

A few weeks passed, and then my dad learned from Jim that the lab found gold in the samples we collected, but there was not enough to make it profitable for a full-scale mining operation. I guess you could say that this was a victory for the spirit of La Cascada.

I found it a struggle to get back into the routine of my studies. I would often catch myself daydreaming about the adventure I shared with my dad. Even today, after nearly 50 years, the spirit of the falls touches me, taking me back to the Dominican Republic and La Cascada!